PSILOCYBIN MUSHROOMS

Forewords

Growing magic mushrooms for consumption is a potentially prohibited practice in some states and countries. The author of this guide doesn't condone or encourage this practice where it is being criminalized. However, the author accepts that people grow and will still grow magic mushrooms and believe it is essential to offer reliable, harm reduction guidelines in order to make people safe. Therefore, this book is intended to guarantee the safety of those who decide to grow and use magic mushrooms.

TABLE OF CONTENTS

INTRODUCTION

The number of people growing magic mushrooms at home is increasing on a daily basis. The home growing of psilocybin removes the risk of misidentifying it in the wild and provides a reliable, year-round supply. It is as well a fun, inexpensive hobby for many growers.

If you do not have an idea of how to grow mushrooms at home, you can begin with a magic mushroom grow kit. These pieces of equipment include a living mycelium substrate (the substance that necessitates the growth of mushroom) that must be kept moist.

It is necessary for you to start from scratch. Making substrate by yourself isn't only more reliable, but if you can do it correctly, it would be less susceptible to contamination. Also, the price difference is not that much and you will ultimately learn a lot more.

This is a reformed system of growing mushrooms indoors. The main idea was to combine vermiculite to a grain-based substrate instead of using only grain. This gives the mycelium additional growing space and mimicking natural conditions. Though this system is a bit more labor-intensive than other methods, often for lesser production, its reliability, low cost, and simplicity makes it suitable for beginners. The process also uses ingredients and materials that are readily available, of which you may already have many of them at home.

CHAPTER ONE: AN OVERVIEW OF PSILICYBIN MUSHROOMS

What Are Psilocybin Mushrooms?

Psilocybin is a hallucinogenic substance that people consume from certain kinds of mushrooms grown in regions of the United States, Mexico, South America, and Europe. The mushrooms that contain psilocybin are generally known as magic mushrooms. Psilocybin is a Schedule – 1 controlled drug; this means it can potentially be abuse, and it doesn't have any legally recognized medical purpose.

People consume psilocybin mushrooms as a recreational drug since it offers euphoria and sensory distortion, commonly found in hallucinogenic drugs, such as LSD. Although psilocybin has not been considered by the medical practitioners to be addictive, consumers may experience worrying hallucinations, panic, and anxiety from taking the drug.

When psilocybin has been ingested and absorbs by the gut, it will be converted to psilocin by the body. The hallucinogenic effects of psilocybin typically take place within thirty minutes of ingestion and stay for about five to six hours. The changes in thought patterns and sensory perception may last for many days in some individuals.

The mushrooms that contain psilocybin are minute and normally tan or brown. People often mistake mushrooms that contain psilocybin for some ordinary mushrooms that are poisonous. Some users typically take psilocybin as a brewed tea or prepare it with a meal to neutralize its bitter taste. Dried mushrooms are usually crushed into powder by the manufacturers and prepared in the form of a capsule. Some individuals will wrap these mushrooms with chocolate and eat.

Facts and Myths on Psilocybin Mushrooms

Facts:

- Psilocybin has both negative and positive psychological and physical effects

- The substance isn't naturally addictive

- Psilocybin can activate psychotic episodes

- A person having a family history of early mental sickness or schizophrenia is vulnerable to an increased adverse psychiatric reaction to psilocybin.

Myths:

There are several myths about psilocybin mushrooms. For example, many people think that magic mushrooms are safer and provide a milder trip compared to other hallucinogenic. In reality, just like other drugs, magic mushroom effects are unpredictable. There have been reports that some people experience more intense and frightening hallucinations on psilocybin mushrooms than on LSD.

Some people also mistake fly agarics mushroom with magic mushrooms – but they aren't the same. Fly agarics mushrooms have psychoactive substances such as muscimol and ibotenic acid known to cause dizziness, delirium, sweating, vomiting, drooling, and twitching.

Magic mushroom's Tolerance, Dependence, and Withdrawal

As it's applicable to most drugs, people tend to develop more tolerance as they use magic mushrooms more often. Also, tolerance increases rapidly with regular use. That is, more of the substance is needed to achieve the same effect.

Developing a tolerance may be somewhat unsafe with psilocybin as taking a large amount can lead to overdose symptoms, which if not severe, can include muscle weakness, diarrhea, seizure, psychosis, panic, or paranoia, vomiting, and agitation.

How Long Does Psilocybin Stay in Your System?

The short-term effects of psilocybin mushroom usually wear-off in six to twelve hours. However, long-term changes in flashbacks and personality can be experienced by the users long after consuming the substances.

On average, the psilocybin half-life varies from one to two hours, and it takes typically 5-6 half-lives for a chemical to be eliminated from your system. The usual urine drug test doesn't check for psilocybin, but people can order specific tests to check for the potent hallucinogen. Magic mushrooms, like several other drugs, can be found in hair follicles for about ninety days.

Addiction

Magic mushrooms are neither addictive and nor do they result in compulsive use. The reason is that, to some extent, the substance can lead to an intense "trip."

Individuals can also build a tolerance to psilocybin quite rapidly, making it difficult to feel any effect after many days of regular intake.

Withdrawal

As there are rare reports of physical withdrawal symptoms from users after discontinuing taking the substance, several people undergo psychological effects such as depression.

The Extent of Use

In the United States, it was suggested by the National Survey on Drug Use and Health that, between 2009 and 2015, approximately 8.5% of the populace reported using magic mushrooms at some point in their life. People usually consume psilocybin at dance clubs or in a set of people in search of inspirational spiritual experience.

In medical settings, medical practitioners have tested magic mushrooms for treating depression, end-stage cancer anxiety, cluster headaches, and other anxiety disorders. Nevertheless, scientists have questioned its safety and effectiveness as a curative measure.

Street Names for Psilocybin

Most of the drug dealers don't sell magic mushroom under its genuine name. Instead, they sell the drug as:

- Magic mushrooms

- Sacred mushrooms

- Shrooms

- Mushies

- Boomers

- Zoomers

- Little smoke

- Simple Simon

- Mushroom soup

- Cubes

- Purple passion

Psilocybin as a Treatment for Depression

There are continuing discussions about whether psilocybin and related hallucinogens can be used to treat depression by psychological specialists.

Two recent studies examined magic mushrooms as a treatment. The first study looked into the psilocybin's ability to lessen the symptoms of depression without having to dull emotions. The second study appraised the connection between any positive therapeutic results and the nature of magic mushrooms-induced hallucinations. Although many researchers are examining some therapeutic uses for magic mushrooms, they still regard psilocybin as illegal and unsafe.

Risks of Using Psilocybin

- Those that are consuming magic mushrooms in an uncontrolled environment may involve in irresponsible behavior, for example, driving while intoxicated.

- Several people might undergo persistent, distressing changes to their impression of the world. These side effects can be visually observed and may stay from weeks to years after taking the drug.

- Doctors now diagnose this condition as hallucinogen persisting perception disorder (HPPD); it is also called a flashback. A flashback is a traumatic recollection of a disconcerting experience. The memory of this traumatic experience in the course of hallucinogen use will result in a bad feeling or a hallucination of distress.

- Many people undergo more unpleasant effects than

hallucinations, for example, agitation, fear, psychosis, delirium, confusion, and syndromes, similar to schizophrenia, which require visiting the emergency room.

- In several cases, a physician would treat these effects using a drug like benzodiazepines. These side effects usually recur in six to eight hours as the effects of the medication fade out.

- Lastly, though the risk may be minute, some users of psilocybin risk inadvertent poisoning by mistakenly consuming a poisonous mushroom. Mushroom poisoning symptoms might include delirium, confusion, and muscle spasms. If you experience any of these symptoms, consult the emergency room immediately.

Because hallucinogenic and other poisonous mushrooms are prevalent in our surroundings, we must learn to frequently remove all mushrooms from neighborhoods where kids are usually present to prevent them from consuming them accidentally. Most accidental intake of mushroom leads to minor gastrointestinal infection, with only the most severe conditions that will call for medical attention.

Abuse Potential

Magic mushroom isn't chemically addictive, and when you stop using it, no physical symptoms will occur. Nevertheless, the routine use of psilocybin can result in individuals becoming tolerant to its effects. Cross-tolerance also takes place with other drugs, such as mescaline and LSD. Individuals who ingest these drugs should wait for quite a few days between doses to undergo the full effect. After many days of taking psilocybin, people may perhaps undergo psychological withdrawal and find it difficult to adjust to reality.

Side Effects of Psilocybin

Magic mushrooms can alter reality and affect mental health. The effects of psilocybin are generally similar to those of LSD. They include altered perception of time and space and intense changes in mood and feeling. Possible effects of psilocybin include:

- Peacefulness

- Euphoria

- Quickly changing emotions

- Spiritual awakening

- Depersonalization or an illusory sense of being disconnected from your environment

- De-realization or the feeling that your environments aren't real

- Visual distortion and alteration, such as halos of light and vivid colors

- Distorted thinking

- Dizziness

- Dilated pupils

- Impaired concentration

- Drowsiness

- Muscle weakness

- Lack of coordination

- Nausea

- Yawning

- Paranoia

- Confusion

- Vomiting

- Unusual body sensations

- Frightening hallucinations

The effects of magic mushrooms vary on individuals based on the disparities in the personality and mental state of the consumer and the immediate environment. If a perso n who uses psilocybin for recreational purposes feels anxious about using it or experiencing mental health problems, his risk of having a bad experience is higher. The most frequently reported adverse event after recreational use of magic mushrooms is psychological distress. This distress may be in the form of short-term psychosis or extreme anxiety.

Signs of Use

If someone close to you uses magic mushrooms, he or she may be nauseous or paranoid or nervous. When it comes to drug use, it is imperative to note any changes in eating patterns or sleeping as well as shifts in personality, mood, and social activities.

How to Get Help

If you suspect your teenager is regularly taking or experimenting psilocybin, think about having a stiff yet affectionate discussion with him or her concerning the risks of psychedelics, especially when taken together with other drugs or alcohol. At the same time, you should let them realize that you're there to help them.

If you have a close relation struggling with substance use or addiction, do not hesitate to call National Helpline at 1-800-662-4357 of the Substance Abuse and Mental Health Services Administration for info on help and treatment facilities in your neighborhood.

CHAPTER TWO: A BRIEF HISTORY OF MAGIC MUSHROOMS

A number of historians viewed that people might have used magic mushrooms as far back as 9000 B.C. in North African native society. These beliefs were based on representations in the paintings of rock, statues, and other objects, which seem like mushrooms found in Aztec and Mayan ruins in Central America. A substance called teonanacati, which means "fresh of gods," which was used by the Aztecs and several other people was psilocybin mushrooms. Alongside morning glory seeds, peyote, and other naturally occurring psychotropics, psilocybin was used to produce vision, induce a trance, and converse with the gods.

In the 16th century, when the Spanish Catholic disciples came into existence, many of them wrote about these psychotropic and their use. Nevertheless, there are several controversies on the thought that psilocybin has a long, sacred history. Many people believe that none of the proof is convincing and that people see what they want to see in the manuscripts, sculptures, and prehistoric paintings. There is confirmed use of magic mushrooms among many present-day tribes of native peoples in Central America, including the Zapatec, Nauhua, Mixtec, and Mazatec.

The Westerners started eating psilocybin in the late 1950s. R. Gordon Wasson, a mycologist (a person who studies mushrooms), embarked on a journey to Mexico to study mushrooms in 1955. He witnessed and took part in a ritual ceremony using psilocybin. A Shaman of the Mazatec organized the ceremony, a native people of the Oaxaca province of Southern Mexico. Gordon wrote an article about his discoveries, and this was published in 1957 in Life Magazine. The title, "Seeking the Magic Mushrooms" was then coined by an editor, in which the article was the source of the phrase. Gordon did not use the title, though. Roger Heim, one of Gordon's colleagues, had solicited the help of Albert Hofmann (the "father" of LSD), who segregated and extorted psilocin and psilocybin from the mushrooms Gordon and Roger brought back from Mexico.

Timothy Leary, a famous advocate for psychotropic drugs i.e., LSD, read the article on Life magazine and was intrigued. He started experimenting with them at Harvard University. There on, magic mushroom turned into mysterious tied to the hippy group. And for the rest of the decade, it became the search for a new form of spirituality. For several years, mushrooms were often connected with the counterculture.

But in recent times, mystical fungi are seeking full acceptance in modern civil society. Many people have adopted what is known as "micro-dosing" with psilocybin, basically ingesting little amounts of the substance. They do not undergo complete trips. Rather, they notice a boost in mood and inspiration, which they think reduces their anxiety and makes them more productive. Their claims seem to be supported by some studies.

Researchers are currently looking for several ways of exploring these inexplicable chemicals. In the 1970s, a ban was placed on magic mushrooms with the exception of medical research, which lately started again after over 3 decades. In October 2018, the Food and Drug Administration (FDA) gave partial authorization to study psilocybin as a cure for depression. The scientists intend to merge magic mushrooms with intense therapy to find improved means of combating treatment-resistant depression, which was said to affect more than one hundred million people globally.

In September 2019, a Center for Psychedelic and Consciousness Research was unveiled at the Johns Hopkins University. The researcher at the University intends to evaluate magic mushrooms as a potential treatment for a number of ailments such as Lyme disease, opioid addiction, alcohol and nicotine addiction, post-traumatic stress disorder, and more.

A lot of researchers across the globe are still finding the potential medicinal use of mystical substances. All of them aim at unlocking how psilocybin and their composites interact with human bodies and brains. Possibly, their outcome would change our perception towards mushrooms; in ways we are yet to imagine.

CHAPTER THREE: LEGAL STANDS OF MAGIC MUSHROOMS

The legal stand of growing, possessing, selling, or taking psilocybin mushrooms depends on where you reside. Magic mushroom is a Schedule I drug in the United States, under the Psychotropic Substance Act as amended. This implies that the drug currently has no medically accepted use, has a high potential for abuse, and is unsafe for use even under a physician's direction. People usually interpret mushrooms as illegal because psilocybin in magic mushrooms is a psychotropic substance. Nevertheless, because mushroom spores do not have psilocybin, many people have pointed this out as vagueness in the federal law.

Typically, busts that have to do with magic mushrooms happen under state law, and nearly all states ban their possession, although states and cities have started reevaluating magic mushrooms. In 2019, Denver was the first city in the United States to legalize psilocybin mushroom, Oakland, and Santa Cruz, California also did same. With these earlier victories, psilocybin legalization advocates are working relentlessly in other states and cities.

Lawmakers in California, Iowa, and Oregon have introduced bills in support of mushrooms legalization.

 Possessing and selling mushroom spores and fresh mushrooms is still legally allowed in many places across the globe. But there are wild inconsistencies in the laws from one nation to another. For instance, until 2005, selling fresh psilocybin mushroom was authorized in Great Britain, and possession of spore is still permitted. The Netherlands, famous as a breeding ground for illegal drugs somewhere else, placed a ban on the sale of dry mushrooms in 2001 and fresh ones in 2018. But the county still allows you to possess a small quantity of "magic truffles," which is magic mushrooms that are not fully mature, thereby eluding the law. In Mexico, unless they are used for religious purposes, there are outright bans of mushrooms. Mushrooms are legalized in Spain, but the authorities frown at seeing grow kits around.

It might be lawful to possess them in some countries but unlawful to sell them. And the punishment for possessing mushroom in other countries can be severe. For example, in Indonesia, the authorities often give death sentences for individuals who are in possession of these kinds of drugs.

Other countries do not have an interest in penalizing or policing mushrooms users or growers. For example, in Brazil, Bahamas, and Jamaica, mushrooms are absolutely legal. Some countries make exemptions to the bans on psilocybin mushrooms when used by native tribes in religious ceremonies; an example of such countries is Mexico.

CHAPTER FOUR: HOW TO IDENTIFY MAGIC MUSHROOMS

For you to avoid mushrooms poisoning, it's imperative to familiarize yourself with different kinds of mushrooms to distinguish between the safe and unsafe ones. This chapter helps you with the descriptions of some of the most familiar types of magic mushrooms, and this will help make sure you experience a safe, reliable trip always. Here are the descriptions of some of the common magic mushrooms:

1. Psilocybe Cubensis

Psilocybe cubensis, also known as "Golden Teacher," are the most popular types of magic mushrooms. They can commonly be found across the Northern region of South America, Central America, and the Southeastern United States. They also grow throughout Southeast Asia countries such as Cambodia, India, Vietnam, and Thailand.

These mushrooms have large caps of diameter between 20-80 mm. The shape of the caps will be conic at an early stage and flatten out when mature. They have a unique reddish, almost cinnamon color. Golden teachers reach their largest size two months before the hottest season of the year. In the U.S., they are commonly found between May and June, though you can still find them up until January.

2. Psilocybe Cyanescens

These types of mushrooms are also called "Wavy Caps." They're typically found in Central Europe, Western Europe, North America, New Zealand, and some regions of the Middle East. Unlike Mexicana and semilanceata, Psilocybe cyanescens have large, wavy caps, with a diameter of between15-50 mm. The color of these mushrooms will be chestnut-brown or caramel when still moist and, will turn to slightly yellowish when they are dry. These mushrooms love growing among wood chips, especially around the edge of urban mulched plants.

3.Psilocybe Semilanceata

Due to the large caps of these mushrooms, they are also called "Liberty Caps." Psilocybe semilanceata is among the most potent magic mushrooms. They're characterized by their pale, curved stems, and leathery-brown caps. The diameter of these mushrooms' caps is between 5-22 mm and a length of approximately 6-22 mm. Their shape can be either conical or bell. The color of their caps varies, from dark shades of brown to a blue or greenish tinge, depending on their hydration.

Psilocybe semilanceata is commonly found both in Europe and North American. They don't grow directly out of dung like a few other mushrooms; but they usually thrive in meadows and pastures.

4.Psilocybe Mexicana

Psilocybe Mexicana mushrooms are also known as "teonanacatl." They commonly grow in South and Central America, where they have been used for a spiritual ceremony for centuries by indigenous tribes. Psilocybe Mexicana and Psilocybe semilanceata are very similar in appearance. They typically have large caps of about 10-20 mm and with a bell or conical shape. Their color is usually light brown.

5. Psilocybe Azurescens

Psilocybe azurescens mushrooms are also called "Flying Saucer Mushroom." These magic mushrooms are very potent because they contain the highest psychoactive biochemical, psilocin, and psilocybin. Studies found that azurescens often grow along a small district of the West Coast of the U.S., and they love growing in dune grasses between September and January.

Psilocybe azurescens usually have large, saucer-like caps with a diameter of 30-100 mm. Their colors remain caramel brown or chestnut when moist and tend to change to dark-blue when mature.

6. Psilocybe Baeocystis

Psilocybe baeocystis is also known as "knobby tops," "bottle caps, "olive caps, or "bluebells." They're typically found across the Pacific Northwest in the United States. They like to grow in wood chips, moldy conifer mulch, and lawns with high lignin content. They occasionally also grow from fallen cones of Douglas fir. These mushrooms can usually be found in fall to early winter.

Psilocybe baeocystis typically have medium-sized caps with a conical shape and have a distinctive color of a dark, olive-brown tone. They usually also have long, straight, or curved stems, which are white-chalk in look.

CHAPTER FIVE: HOW TO GROW PSILOCYBIN MUSHROOMS INDOOR

What Type Should You Grow?

As a beginner, it is recommended that you choose Psilocybe cubensis B+, also known as Golden Teacher mushrooms. This variety is among the most popular and not as potent as some other species. So, it is ideal for beginners.

The Material You Will Need

Ingredients

- Vermiculite, medium/fine

- Organic brown rice flour

- Spore syringe, 10 - 12 cc

- Clean drinkable water

Equipment

- 12 half-pint glass jars (without shoulder) with lids (for example, canning jars)

- Small nail and hammer

- Bowl for mixing

- Strainer

- Measuring cup

- Heavyweight tin foil

- Small towel (or about. 10 paper towels)

- Large cooking pan with a tight-fitting lid, for steaming

- Micropore tape

- Clear plastic storage container, 50-115L

- Mist spray bottle

- Drill with a 1/4-inch drill bit

- Perlite

Hygiene Supplies

- Propane/ butane torch lighter

- Rubbing alcohol

- Air sanitizer

- Surface disinfectant

- Surgical mask (optional)

- Latex gloves (sterilized) optional

- Still air or glove box (optional)

Spore Syringes: A right spore syringe is one thing you may find challenging to get. This syringe will hold your psilocybin spores, and it will be used to "sow" them into the substrate. A number of cultivators have reported problems of misidentified strains, contamination, and even syringes containing only water. Nevertheless, if you search thoroughly and find a reliable seller, you will not have any issues. Moreover, when you have successfully grown your first batch of psilocybin, you can begin filling your own syringes.

Instructions:

This method is super simple: Prepare your water, vermiculite, and brown rice flour substrate and share it among the disinfected jars. Bring in spores and allow the mycelium to develop. This is the arrangement of threads that will strengthen the growth of your mushroom. After four to five weeks, move your inhabited substrate to a fruiting grow chamber and wait for your mushroom to thrive in there.

Note: It is essential to ensure hygiene prior to starting: Brush your teeth, take a shower, wear a clean cloth, sterilize your surfaces and equipment, spray your surroundings with an air sanitizer, and so on. You do not need ample space, but your environment must be well sterile. Some molds and bacteria can quickly proliferate where mushrooms are being grown, so it is essential to reduce the risk.

First Step: Preparation

1. Prepare the Jars:

- Get the nail and hammer ready by wiping them with alcohol to sterilize them, create four holes through each of the lids, equally spaced around their perimeters

2. Prepare the Substrate:

- For each of the jars, carefully mix 1/4 cup of water and 2/3 cup of vermiculite in a large bowl. Drain surplus water with the sterile strainer.

- Add 1/4 cup of brown rice flour for each half-pint glass jar to the mixing bowl and mix with the wet vermiculite.

3. Fill the Jars:

- It is important to be cautious not to pack too tightly, fill the jars to reach a half-inch of the rims. Then use rubbing alcohol to sterilize the top half-inch.

- Fill up the jars with a layer of dry vermiculite so that the substrate is insulated from contaminants.

4. Steam Disinfect:

- Firmly screw the lids and use a tin foil to cover the jar. To prevent condensation and water from getting through the holes, secure the foil's edges around the jars' sides.

- Put the paper towels or small towel inside the large cooking pan and position the jars on top. Make sure the jars do not touch the bottom.

- Pour clean running water into the pot to a level halfway up the jars' sides and apply low heat to give it a slow boil, making sure the jars stay straight in the pot.

- Put the tight lid on the cooking pan and wait to steam for seventy-five to ninety minutes. Refill with boiling clean water if the pot runs dry.

Note: Some cultivators prefer using a pressure cooker set for sixty minutes at 15 PSI.

5. Leave to Cool:

- When the steaming process is completed, let the jars remain in the pot overnight or for some hours. They ought to be at room temperature before proceeding to the next stage.

Second Step: Inoculation

1. Disinfect and Prepare syringe:

- Heat the length of your syringe's needle with a lighter until it turns red hot. Leave to cool and use alcohol to wipe it, ensuring your hands do not touch the needle.

- Pull back the plunger slightly and shiver the syringe to distribute the spores of magic mushroom evenly.

Note: if the needle and spore syringe needed to be assembled before use, it is vital to avoid contamination during the process. Disinfected surgical mask and latex gloves may help out, but it is best to assemble the syringe in a sterile glove box or still air.

2. Inject Spores:

- Take away the foil from the first of the glass jars and insert the syringe through one of the holes. Allow the needle to touch the jar's side, inject about ¼ cc of the spore liquid (or a little less if making use of a ten-cc syringe across the 12-jars)

- Do the same for the remaining 3 holes. Ensure to wipe the needle with alcohol between each.

- Make use of micropore tape to cover the hole and set aside the jar without the foil.

- Replicate the inoculation process for the remaining jars, disinfecting the needle with a lighter and then alcohol between each.

Third Step: Colonization

1. Wait for the Mycelium:

- Move your inoculated jars to a clean and remote place. Avoid temperatures more than 70 to 80°F and direct sunlight.

- You should start seeing white, fluffy-looking mycelium scattering outward from the sites of inoculation between seven and fourteen days.

Note: Be conscious of any sign of infectivity such as smells and colors, and throw away immediately, any jars that you suspect. This should be done outside in a safe bag without having to unscrew the lids. If you are not sure whether a jar has been contaminated or infected, always be cautious and observant, because some contaminants are unsafe for human beings.

2. Consolidate:

- After three to four weeks, you ought to have no less than six fruitfully colonized jars if all walk fine. Wait for an additional 7 days to let the mycelium strengthen its hold on the substrate.

Fourth Step: Prepare the Grow Chamber

1. Make a fruiting chamber:

- Take the plastic storage box and make ¼-inch holes about 2 inches separate all over the base, sides, and lid. Make your holes from the inside out into a block of wood to avoid cracking.

- Place the container over 4 stable objects, put together at the corners to enable the flow of air beneath. You can also cover the surface beneath the container to keep it from the leakage of moisture.

Note: The fruiting chamber is not the only available design, but it is fast and straightforward to prepare, and it makes the right choice for beginners. As you progress, you could opt for other alternatives.

2. Add Perlite:

- Put the perlite inside a strainer and run it under the cold running water to soak.

- Let it drain until no-drip remains. Afterward, spread the perlite over the bottom of your grow chamber.

- Replicate for a layer of perlite about four to five inches.

Fifth Step: Fruiting

1.   Birth   the   Colonized Substrates/Mycelium ("Cake")

- Unseal the jar and take out the dry layer of vermiculite from each of them, ensuring you do not damage the cake during this process.

- Turn over each jar and tap down on a sterile surface to release the cake undamaged.

2. Dunk the Mycelium:

- Rinse the cake one by one under cold running water to get rid of any loose vermiculite, ensuring that they are not damaged.

- Fill a large container or cooking pot with lukewarm water and put the cakes in it. Submerge the cakes just underneath the surface with a heavy item.

- Let the container or pot stay at room temperature for up to twenty-four hours for the cakes to rehydrate.

3. Roll the Cakes:

- Take out the substrate or cake from the water and put them on a sterile surface. And then, fill the mixing container with dry vermiculite.

- Next, roll the cakes one after the other to thoroughly coat them in vermiculite to help retain the humidity.

4. Move the Cakes to Grow Chamber:

- Cut the tin foil into square per each cake, moderately large to contain them without having to touch the perlite. Space the square foil evenly in the grow chamber.

- Next, put the cakes on top of each foil and softly mist the chamber with the spray bottle.

- Use a lid to fan the cakes before closing.

5. Optimize and Watch Conditions:

- To maintain the moisture, mist the chamber about 4 times daily. You'll want to be sure you don't soak your cakes with water.

- Use a lid to fan the cakes for about 6 times daily, especially after every misting, to aid the airflow.

Note: Many gardeners make use of fluorescent lights put on a twelve-hour cycle, but ambient or indirect lighting in the daytime is ideal. Mycelium only requires a touch of light to determine where there is open air and where to spin out mushrooms.

Sixth Step: Harvesting

1. Check for Fruits:

- Your fruits or mushrooms will emerge as tiny white bumps before developing into "pin" They will ready to harvest after five to twelve days.

2. Pick your Fruits:

- To harvest, cut the mushrooms close to the cake. Do not leave your mushrooms to reach the peak of their growth, because they will start losing potency when they are mature.

Note: the most appropriate time to pick mushrooms is right before their veil break. They will have covered gills and light, conical-shaped at this stage.

Storing Psilocybin Mushroom

Magic mushrooms may spoil within a few weeks inside the refrigerator. So, if you intend to preserve them for a longer period, you will need to decide your method of storing them. Drying is the most effective and potent way for long-term storage. It will keep them potent for two to three years provided that you keep them in a cool, dark and dry place. If you store them in the freezer, they will remain potent indefinitely.

One of the methods of drying mushrooms is to place them on a sheet of paper outside for some days, possibly in front of a fan. The issue with this technique is that the mushrooms will not get "cracker dry". This means that when you attempt to bend them, they will not break, which means they will hold some humidity. They might also considerably reduce in efficacy, depending on how long they are left out. The most effective way of drying then is using a dehydrator, but that may be costly.

Using the desiccant below is a good alternative:

- Air-dry your magic mushrooms for forty-eight hours, preferably with a fan

- Next, put a layer of desiccant in the bottom of an airtight container. You can buy desiccants such as anhydrous calcium chloride and silica gel kitty litter from hardware stores.

- Put a wire rack or similar alternative over the desiccant to prevent your psilocybin from touching it.

- Assemble your psilocybin on the wire rack, making sure they aren't too close together. Afterward, seal the container.

- Leave them in the container for some days, and then check if they are cracker dry.

- Once they are cracker dry, move the mushrooms to storage bags (such as vacuum seal or Ziploc) and put them in a freezer.

Reusing the Substrate

After your first flush, you can reuse the same cake for about 3 times. You only need to dry them for some days and follow step 2 of 5 (dunk the substrate). But do not roll the cake in the vermiculite; simply put them in the grow chamber for misting and fanning as usual. If you begin to notice contaminants (typically about the 3rd reuse), soak the cakes using the mister spray and throw them away in a safe bag.

How to Make Spore Syringes

- The first thing you need to do is taking a spore print from a full-grown mushroom, that is, the one that grows until its top has opened out, and the edges have turned upside down. On such mushroom, you will see a buildup of dark purple deposits around its bottom. The deposits are the psilocybin spores.

- To collect them, take out the cap with a glow-sterilized knife and put it gills down on a disinfected sheet of paper. Next, cover the collected spore with a sterile jar or glass for 24 hours to prevent it from the air. Then, place the spore print out in an airtight plastic bag.

- To fill the syringe with spore, scratch some of the spore print into a disinfected glass of distilled water.

This can be bought at auto supply stores. Next, fill the sterile syringe and unfilled it back into the glass many times so that the spores will be evenly distributed. Once the spore is thoroughly mixed with water, fill the syringe the last time and put it in an airtight plastic bag. Leave the syringe at room temperature for some days for the spores to hydrate. Afterward, refrigerate the syringe until you are ready to use it. You can use it within two months.

CHAPTER SIX: TIPS AND ADVICE FOR SAFE USE OF MAGIC MUSHROOMS☐

Before the Trip:

- To experience a safe trip when you use psilocybin mushrooms, it is recommended that you always plan your trip at least a few days ahead so that you can be physically and mentally prepared for the mind-altering experience. You have to take specific safety measures, especially if you are taking magic mushrooms for the time.

- Eighteen years is the minimum age for anyone to start using psilocybin. Naturally, everybody doesn't mature the same pace, which is the reason the use of magic mushrooms is recommended to people of 21 years above.

- Use mushrooms only when you're in good mental health, i.e., do not use it when you are depressed. It is also imperative that you're in good physical health, that is, you don't have viral or bacterial infections such as the flu or common cold.

- Don't take psilocybin if you're alone. Preferably, take mushrooms with someone that is experienced.

- Use psilocybin mushrooms only once in a month. After consuming mushroom, wait for a month in order to achieve the same effect. Taking mushrooms within a shorter period tends to lessen their impact.

- Ensure that there is enough drinking water for everyone. It is recommended that sugar-containing drinks should also be available. This is what you need in case you want to reduce the effects.

- The best effect is experienced when magic mushrooms are taken on an empty stomach. Use psilocybin no less than 2 hours 30 minutes after your last meal. Depending on your metabolism rate, be expecting the effects to begin within thirty to fifty minutes.

- A portion of the cubensis species is 15 grams. In dry weight, this is 2 grams. Never take more than this. Not even when your friends already feel the effects, and you don't. Just wait a little longer.

- To ascertain the exact amount of dried cubensis that makes the right portion, try to weigh a portion of 30grams of fresh cubensis for example, and allow it to dry. Next, weigh this portion again once it has dried. The weight of this portion of dry cubensis is automatically equal to 30grams of its fresh counterpart. So, the dosage for dried cubensis is about 4grams per portion for an experienced user and 2 grams, which is half of 4grams is recommended for a beginner.

- Take mushrooms amid people you like and trust, not strangers. Do not consume psilocybin because others are using it or because they persuade you to do so while you are not really confident of its potential effects. Use it because you want to use it.

- Ensure there are one or more people in your midst that will not take mushrooms so they will be able to take care of anyone that needs attention.

- Stay out of appointments for the next 24 hours after taking magic mushrooms. It is best to stay indoors, especially if you're taking it for the first time. Make sure your phone is switched off because most people tend to irrationally react when they're faced with good or bad news. You are as well advised to switch off your doorbell to avoid disturbances. Psilocybin is not a party drug. Concert halls or festivals aren't the ideal places to use it.

- Ensure to know how you can contact the local emergency services in your area.

- On no account should you use magic mushrooms with other drugs, cannabis or alcohol.

During the Trip:

Drink a lot of water. No matter how nice the effects of psilocybin are, your body system identifies the active chemicals as toxins. Water will help remove these substances from your system. Warning: Don't think that the effects will be intensified or stay longer if you don't drink water. The bodies will just take it somewhere else in your system as the primary concern will be the removal of these toxins. And as a result, you will be dehydrated, and this can be very hazardous. You will experience the trip of the same duration and strength anyway.

Do not use alcohol or other drugs before, during, or after your trip. This is so important that I repeat this statement. One of the mushroom's effects is that it makes your mind jumps in high speed from one thought to another. Your reaction's speed is decelerated by alcohol and will cause your thought to start to run in loops. This is awfully unpleasant and could quickly result in a bad trip. Also, when using alcohol, you are prone to dehydration.

The Journey

Settle down and follow where they take you. Magic mushroom effects are breathtaking. This implies that once you are intoxicated, your senses function on a higher frequency. You'll experience things that you ordinarily wouldn't realize or see. These hallucinations are usually enigmatic and aren't always what they appear to be. At times, the experience can be scary, but just put up with it and do not attempt to fight it. Stopping it may work against you.

Needs

Human beings are different due to our diverse backgrounds. As people are not alike, our needs will not be the same when we are tripping. Some people love to be silent; others prefer to chat. While someone wants to make love, another does not want anybody to touch him or her. Communicating about this earlier will make you understand the significance of surrounding yourself with the people you trust and like.

Waves

The magic mushrooms effects appear and go in waves. And it is also applicable to how a person experiences the strength of the trip. At a particular point in your trip, you may feel that the effects are wearing off. Don't because of that take more doses to boost the effects. After a while, you will discover the effects will intensify without taking additional doses.

In Case of a Bad Trip

When you follow the above tips and advice strictly, it will significantly minimize your chances of having a bad trip. Nevertheless, it may happen that someone in your midst did not take the instruction strictly. Once someone has a bad trip, you'll notice that such a person will begin to react very nervously, extremely paranoid, or even violent or hysterical. The ideal thing is for the person that doesn't take mushrooms should comfort him or her.

Caution:

- On no account should you lose a person with a bad trip out of sight. Such a person may suddenly attempt to take off, so don't leave him alone.

- Look for a calm place where this person can lie down or sit. Allow such an individual to focus on breathing peacefully.

- Get him or her sweet things to drink and, if possible, to eat as well. A high dosage of vitamin C (1mg) can also help.

- The effects of the substance will gradually begin to get milder after a couple of minutes.

- A bad trip usually will stay just as long as a normal trip. The person experiencing a bad trip may feel that it will never end. Give them comfort by convincing them that it will all be soon come to an end. Making them drink sweet beverages (such as fruit juice) will help reduce the time-span of the trip.

- If you think you have done all your best for the person and after a while, he or she is getting uncontrollable, you should get in contact with the emergency services. In the U.S, their number is 911 and 112 in Europe. Be absolutely sincere to the services in what the victim is going through and what he or she has used as intoxicants.

CHAPTER SEVEN: DIFFERENT WAYS TO SAFELY CONSUME MAGIC MUSHROOMS

Most people consume psilocybin mushrooms for two significant reasons: either as a spiritual rite or for fun. Magic mushrooms can surely be pleasurable at lower doses, leading to a pleasant, mind-broadening trip experience. Some people regard magic mushrooms as a key to the doors of perception – these set of people usually consume higher doses. With the right guidance, knowledge, and experience, this substance could lead you to useful insights into the surrounding world, reality wherein you exist, and the one beyond. Whatever your motives for using magic mushrooms, as a beginner, do not consume a large amount at a time.

1. Chew and Swallow

Eating magic mushrooms is the usual way of ingesting them. When using this method, ensure to chew them well to bring out all the juices. The psychoactive chemicals discharged from the mushroom through your saliva will begin to mix with your blood and get to every of your body's cells. It will take approximately thirty to fifty minutes to begin to work, depending on the amount you eat and your body metabolism.

To avoid the chewing part unpleasant taste, you can crush the truffles with a truffle grinder and swallow the paste. With this, you will not feel the flavor more than necessary.

2. Make a Cup of Mushroom Tea

Consuming your psilocybin in the form of a tea will get rid of the unpleasant taste. Boil a cup of water, cut the mushroom amount you desire to take into bits, and put them inside the water. Heat the pot over low heat, getting it close to simmering. Don't allow it to boil so that the active compounds are not destroyed. Leave to rest for about ten to fifteen minutes and then drink. If desired, add honey.

3.Make and Use Mushroom Capsules

With capsules, users are offered the option to micro-dose their magic mushrooms. And with a grinder and a capsule machine, you will be able to make magic mushrooms capsules. Mushrooms are known for not being tasty. Fortunately, using capsules take away that moldy flavor and makes dosing easier beyond imagination. Only use your self-made capsules – that is the only way you can be sure of their integrity. It is less suspicious and very easy to carry around some capsules than fresh mushrooms.

When it comes to micro-dosing, the experience can be relatively adapted to through doses. Several people reported taking magic mushrooms in this manner helps them in inspirational pursuits or the people who engage in problems solving. By helping to provide focus, boosting the level of energy, and increasing positivity, the secret to micro-dosing is to keep the quantity of mushrooms below 0.5 g per capsule. Thus, the user will not be overpowered by the effects. Not only that, but you will also understand your level of tolerance better. Therefore, it is best to experiment a little to know what works for you. Don't forget, start low and go slow.

4. Incorporate Your Psilocybin with Edibles

By adding psilocybin to food, you are unlocking an entirely new world of experiences — not only from the mind-broadening trip but also by practicing your culinary skills. Basically, taking magic mushrooms with food will help with the taste and remove the feeling of nausea that most users undergo. Since you can add magic mushrooms to virtually any food, it is left for users to decide base on their favorite. However, if you're stuck for ideas, here are some suggestions for incorporating mushrooms with your edibles:

It is essential to avoid adding mushrooms during the cooking stage. Psilocybin, which is the vital ingredient in mushrooms responsible for the trip, tends to diminish under too much heat. For example, baking mushrooms on top of a pizza can lead to poor tripping experience. It is ideal for adding them to toppings or sauces after the cooking stage.

A perfect example is taking magic mushrooms with honey or adding them to freshly prepared pesto, as you can enjoy both of them cold. Magic chocolate truffles are a popular favorite. Depending on your metabolism rate, the more the mushrooms you take, the longer and healthier the trip will be. Therefore, try to experiment with dosage until you find what is right for you.

As I have stated earlier, mushroom poisoning could be very harmful. Therefore, it's of great importance that you always be extremely cautious when dealing with mushrooms. Don't grow or use a mushroom unless you're sure of its safety. Avoid making hand to mouth contact after you must have handled mushrooms, as this can bring in dangerous contaminants into your system. It is recommended that you spend more time identifying attributes and visual differences between them so you will be reasonably proficient at it prior to consuming any kind of magic mushrooms.